AUG 1 2 2010

2000-2009
BEST COUNTRY SONGS

TEN YEARS OF SHEET MUSIC HITS!

Produced by
Alfred Music Publishing Co., Inc.
P.O. Box 10003
Van Nuys, CA 91410-0003
alfred.com

Printed in USA.

ISBN-10: 0-7390-6882-2
ISBN-13: 978-0-7390-6882-3

 Alfred Cares. Contents printed on 100% recycled paper.

CONTENTS

ALL I ASK FOR ANYMORE

Words and Music by
TIM JAMES and CASEY BEATHARD

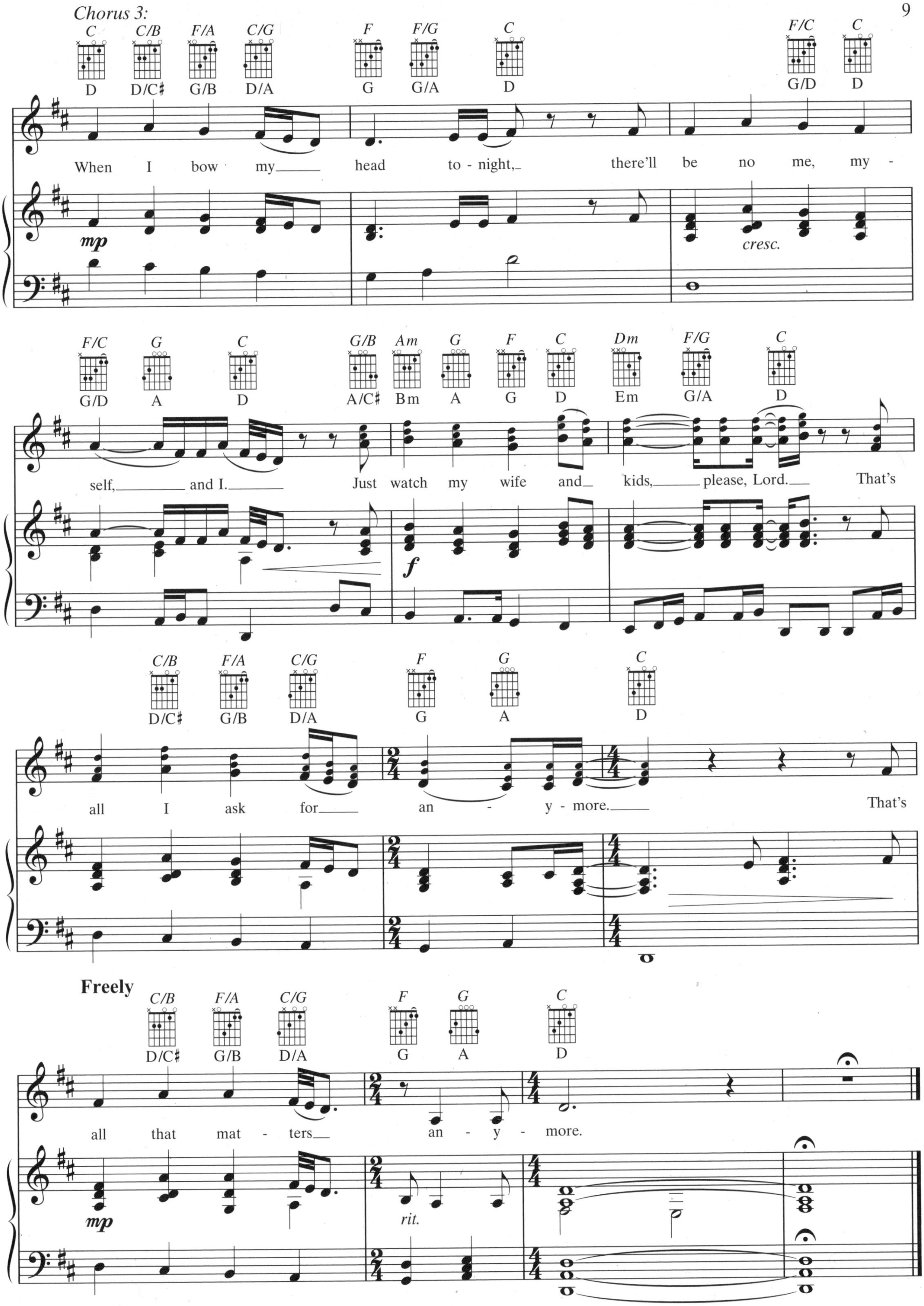

Chorus 3:
C C/B F/A C/G F F/G C F/C C
D D/C# G/B D/A G G/A D G/D D
When I bow my head to-night, there'll be no me, my-
mp
cresc.
F/C G C G/B Am G F C Dm F/G C
G/D A D A/C# Bm A G D Em G/A D
self, and I. Just watch my wife and kids, please, Lord. That's
f
C/B F/A C/G F G C
D/C# G/B D/A G A D
all I ask for an-y-more. That's
Freely
C/B F/A C/G F G C
D/C# G/B D/A G A D
all that mat-ters an-y-more.
mp
rit.

ALL SUMMER LONG

Words and Music by MATTHEW SHAFER, R.J. RITCHIE,
WARREN ZEVON, LEROY MARINELL, WADDY WACHTEL,
ED KING, GARY ROSSINGTON and RONNIE VAN ZANT

14

sum-mer long.

(vocal 2nd time only:) Ah.

(Inst. solo ad lib....

Ah.

Ah.

Ah.

D.S. 𝄋 al Coda

4. Now,
...end solo)

ALL-AMERICAN GIRL

Words and Music by
CARRIE UNDERWOOD, KELLEY LOVELACE
and ASHLEY GORLEY

All-American Girl - 6 - 1

D **A** **D** **A/C#**

lit - tle___ ba - by___ boy.___
se - nior___ foot - ball___ star.___

D **A** **D**

Some - one he could take fish - in',___
Be - fore you knew it, he was drop - pin' pass - es,___

A/C# **D** **A**

throw the foot - ball and be___ his pride___ and___ joy.___
skip - pin' prac - tice just to spend more time___ with___ her.___

D **A/C#** **D** **E** **A/C#**

He could al - read - y see him
The coach said,___ "Hey, son,

hold-in' that tro-phy,___ tak-in' his team to state.___ But when the
what's_ your prob-lem?___ Tell me, have you lost your mind?"___

nurse_ came in with a lit-tle pink blan-ket,___ all those big dreams changed._
Dad-dy said, "You'll lose your free ride_ to col-lege.___ Boy, you'd bet-ter tell her good-

Chorus:

___bye." And_ now he's wrapped_ a-round her fin-ger. She's the
But,_

cen-ter of___ his whole world.___ And his heart be-longs_

ANYWAY

Words and Music by
MARTINA McBRIDE, BRAD WARREN
and BRETT WARREN

al-ways turn out like I think it should, but I do it an-y-way.

I do it an-y-way.

decresc.

Verse 2:

2. This world's gone cra-zy, and it's hard to be-lieve that to-

mor-row will be bet-ter than to-day. Be-lieve it

BEFORE HE CHEATS

Words and Music by
JOSH KEAR and
CHRIS TOMPKINS

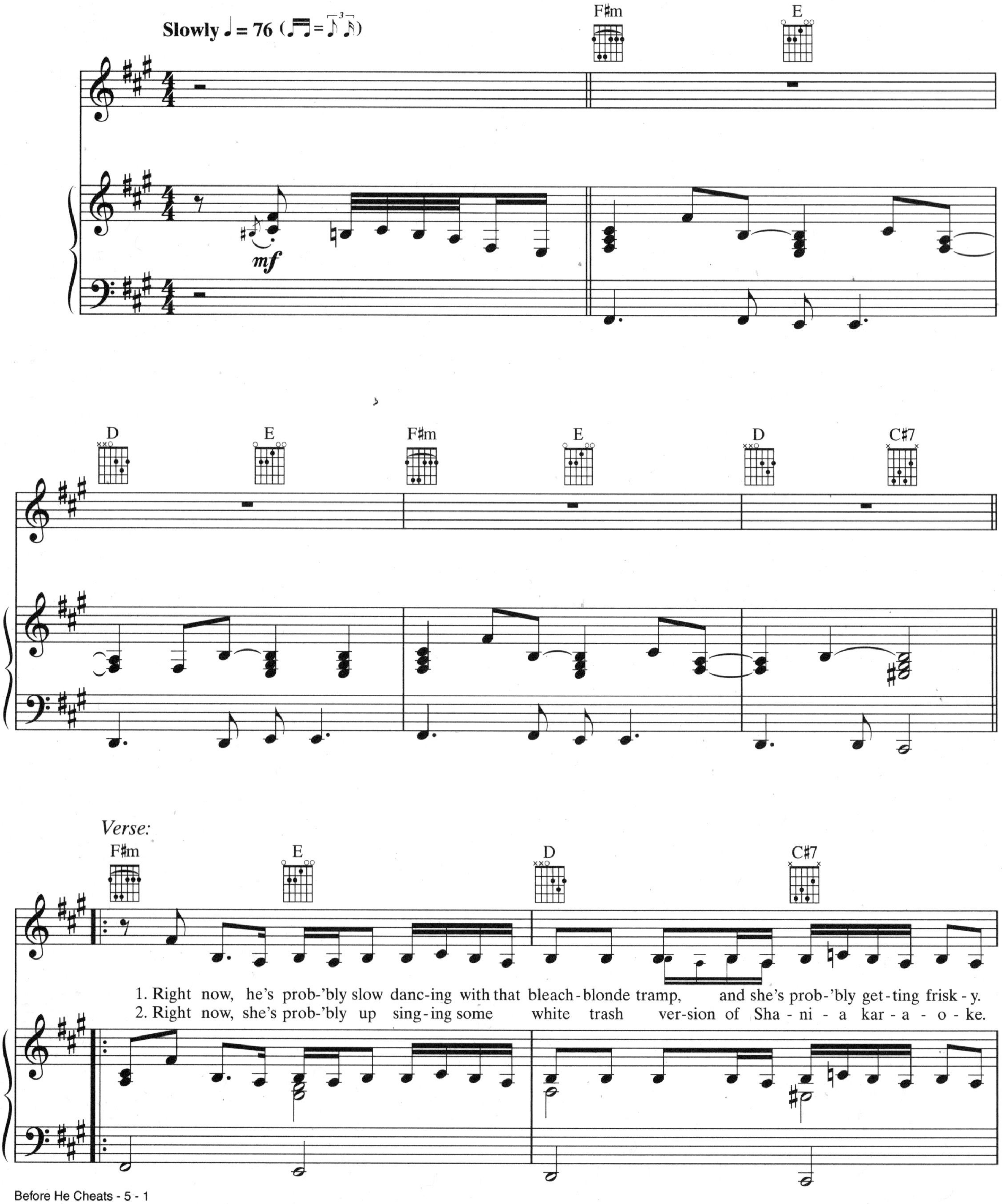

Slowly ♩ = 76

Verse:

1. Right now, he's prob'ly slow danc-ing with that bleach-blonde tramp, and she's prob'ly get-ting frisk-y.
2. Right now, she's prob'ly up sing-ing some white trash ver-sion of Sha-ni-a kar-a-o-ke.

Before He Cheats - 5 - 1

COMIN' TO YOUR CITY

Words and Music by
JOHN RICH and KENNY ALPHIN

Bridge:

L. A.'s got the freaks_ at Pink's and fif - teen - dol - lar drinks,_ and San An -

to - ni - o_____ is a wild, wild ro - de - o._____ And in

Phoe - nix, Ar - i - zo - na, we drank way too much Co - ro - na and we

woke up by the riv - er in Jeff Cit - y, MO._____ And we're

Chorus:

com - in' to your cit - y,___ gon - na

play our gui - tars and sing you a coun - try song.___ We'll all___ be

fly - in' high - er than a jet air - lin - er,___ and if you

1.

want a lit - tle bang in your yin yang, come a - long.___ Yeah, we're

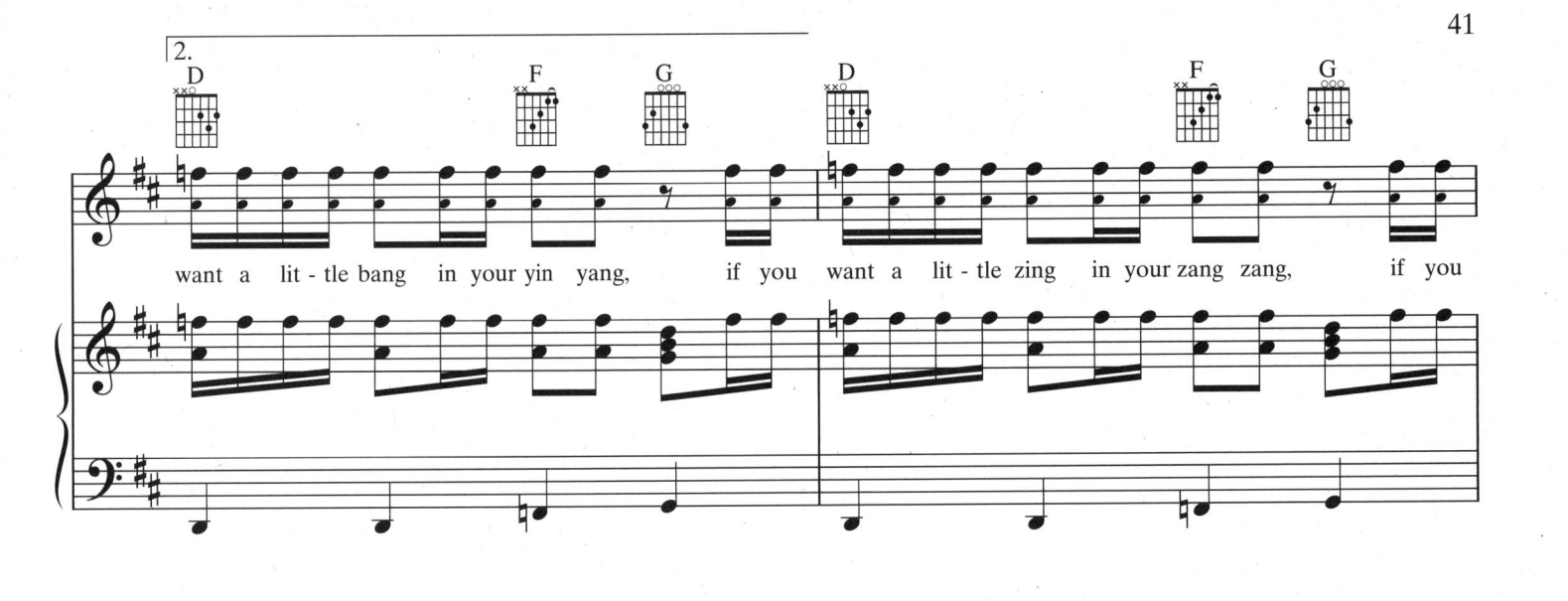

want a lit-tle bang in your yin yang, if you want a lit-tle zing in your zang zang, if you

want a lit-tle ching in your chang chang, come a-long,_____ come a-long, come a-long,

Repeat ad lib. and fade

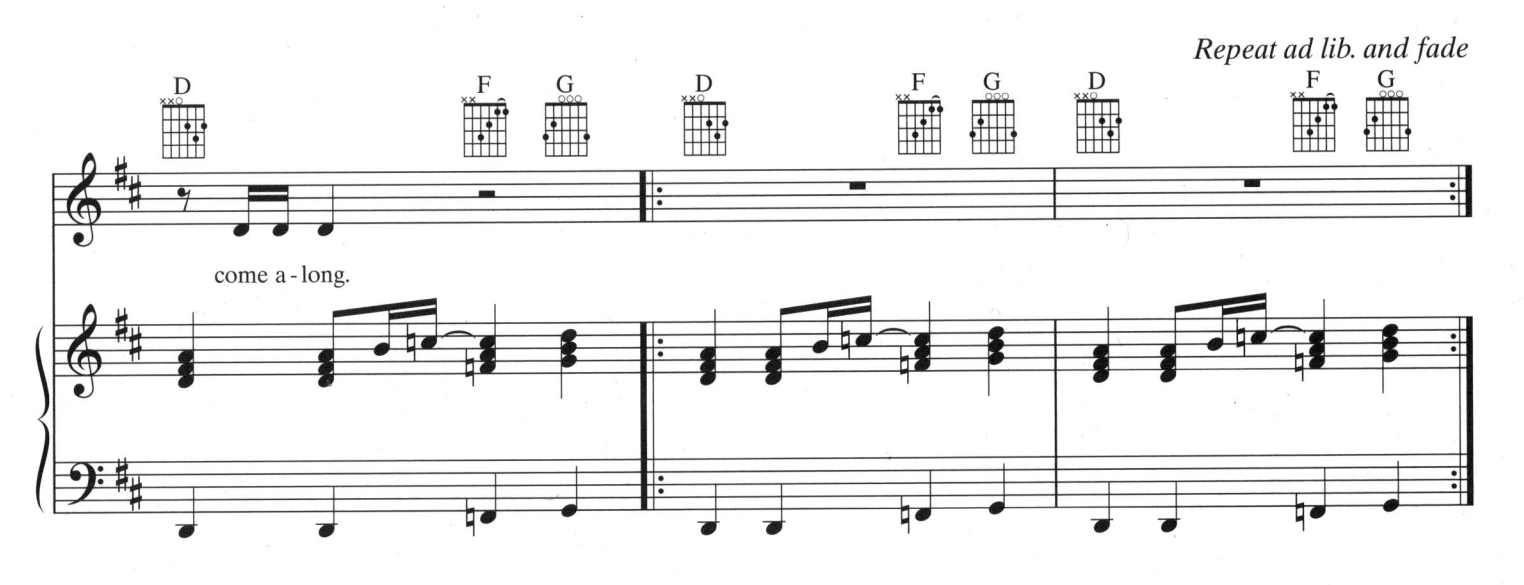

come a-long.

CONSIDER ME GONE

Words and Music by
MARV GREEN and STEVE DIAMOND

44

Chorus:

thing you can't stand to lose,___ if I'm not that ar - row to the heart of you,___

if you don't get___ drunk on my kiss,___ if you think___

you can do bet - ter than this,___ than I guess___ we're done. Let's not drag___ this on.___

[1.

Con - sid - er me gone.___

COWBOY CASANOVA

Gtr. tuned down a whole step:
⑥ = D   ③ = F
⑤ = G   ② = A
④ = C   ① = D

Words and Music by
CARRIE UNDERWOOD, MIKE ELIZONDO
and BRETT JAMES

Cowboy Casanova - 7 - 1

*Play cue notes and chords in parentheses 2nd time.

52

I SAW GOD TODAY

Words and Music by
MONTY CRISWELL, WADE KIRBY
and RODNEY CLAWSON

DO I

Words and Music by
CHARLES KELLEY, DAVE HAYWOOD
and LUKE BRYAN

1. Ba - by, what are we___ be - com - ing? It feels just like we're al - ways run - ning,

roll - ing through the mo - tions ev - 'ry day.___

Do I - 6 - 1

Chorus:

turn you on at all when I kiss_ you, ba - by? Does the sight of me want-ing you drive_ you cra - zy? Do I

have your love? Am I still e-nough? Tell me don't I or tell me do I, ba - by,

give you ev-'ry-thing that you ev - er want - ed? Would you rath-er just turn a-way and leave me lone - ly?

Do I just need_ to give up_ and get on_ with my_ life?_____ Ba - by, do_ I?_

DO YOU BELIEVE ME NOW

Words and Music by
TIM JOHNSON, DAVE PAHANISH
and JOE WEST

Repeat ad lib. and fade

FEEL THAT FIRE

Words and Music by
BRETT WARREN, BRAD WARREN,
BRETT BEAVERS and DIERKS BENTLEY

Moderately slow ♩ = 84

*Recorded in A flat with guitar tuned down a half step.

Feel That Fire - 6 - 1

G

She wants to wear my shirt to bed, she wants to make ev-'ry stray a pet,___ and
She wants to make love on___ a train, some days she on-ly___ wants a break,___

D   A

drive a-round__ in my truck with no place to go.___ But she needs to
she wants what__ she wants,__ and, man, I know,__ I know,__ I know.__ She needs to

𝄋 *Chorus:*

A2   G

feel_____ that fire,_____ the

Bm7   A

one that lets__ her know__ for sure, she's ev-'ry-thing__ I want__ and more. Her

...end solo) She wants her nails paint - ed black,

she wants the toy in the Crack-er Jack, she wants to ride the bull__ at the ro - de - o.__

Repeat ad lib. and fade

Good Morning Beautiful

Words and Music by
TODD CERNEY and ZACK LYLE

Slowly ♩ = 72

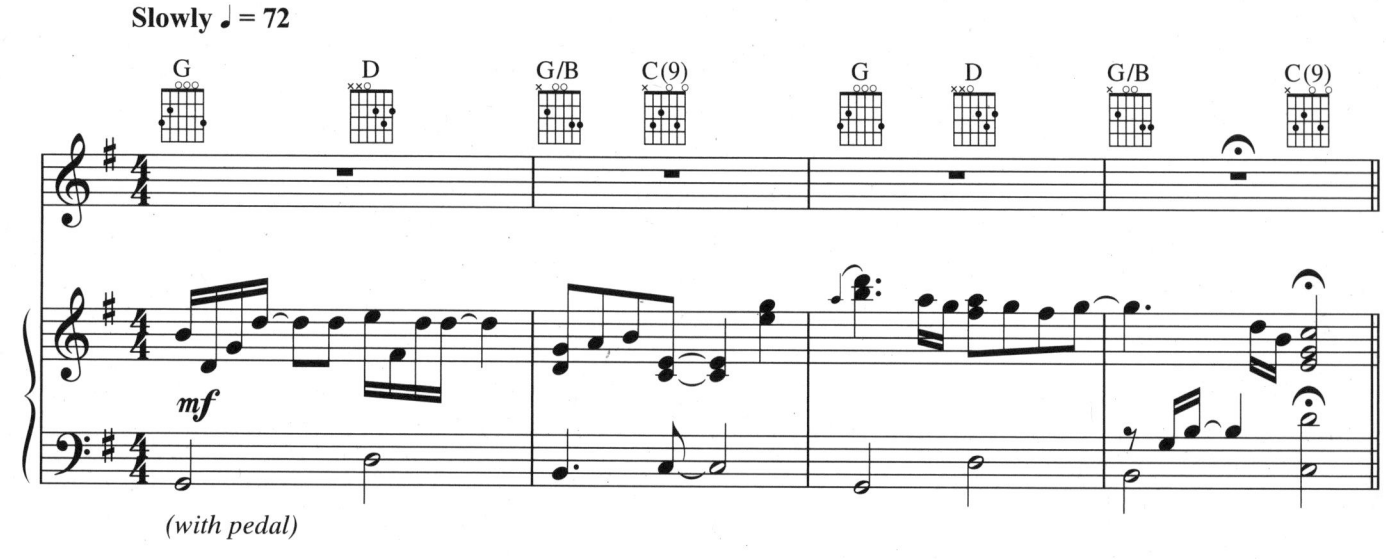

(with pedal)

Chorus:

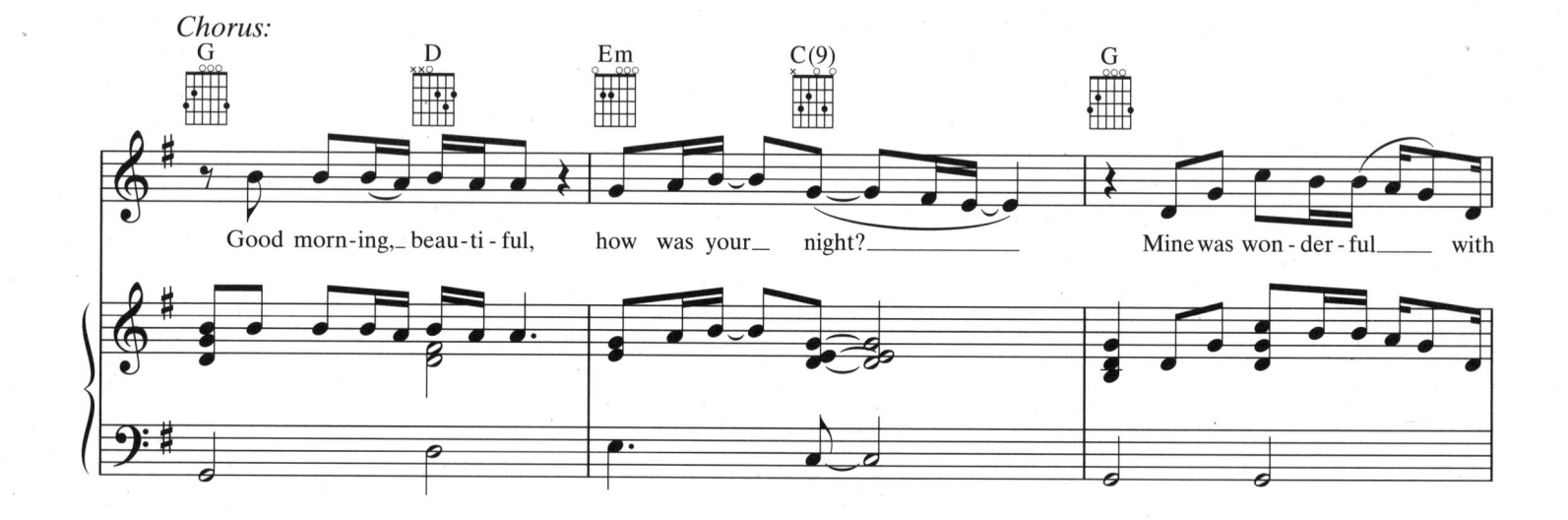

Good morn-ing,_ beau-ti-ful, how was your_ night?_____ Mine was won-der-ful_____ with

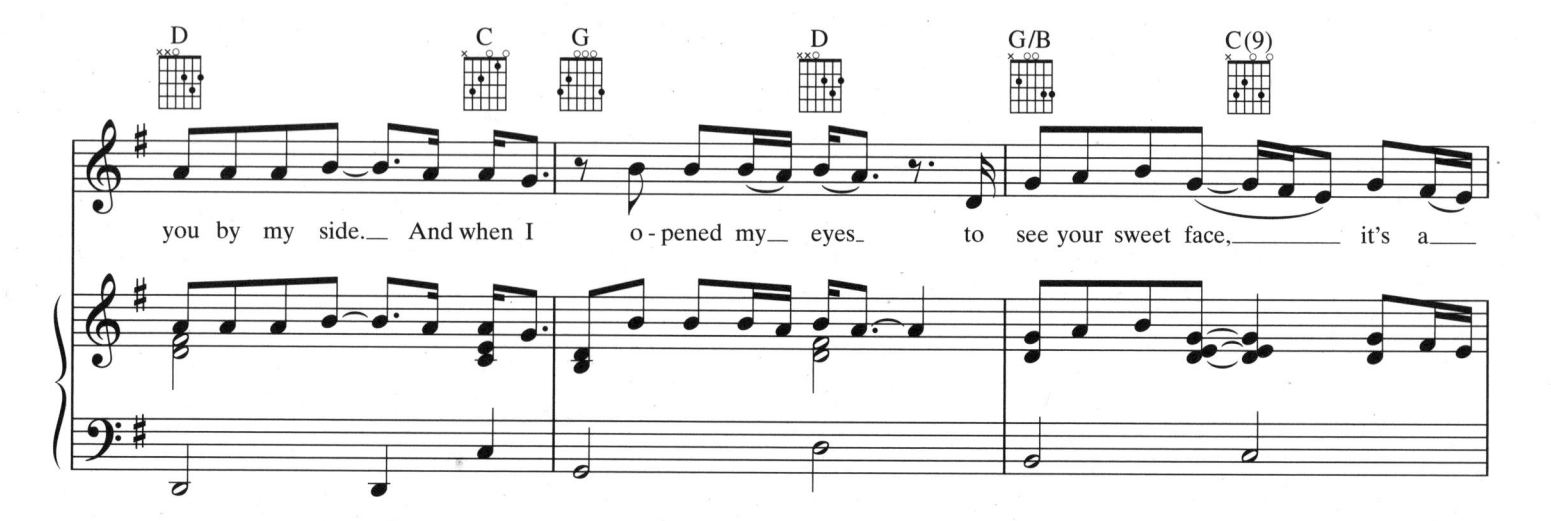

you by my side._ And when I o-pened my_ eyes_ to see your sweet face,_____ it's a_____

Good Morning Beautiful - 4 - 1

THE GOOD STUFF

Words and Music by
JIM COLLINS and CRAIG WISEMAN

The Good Stuff - 6 - 1

D G/A D Am7 G/B C D
y. He said, "You can't find that here. 1. 'Cause it's the
Chorus:
G D/F♯ Em
first long kiss on a sec - ond date, Mom - ma's all wor - ried when you
(2.) See additional lyrics
G7 C G/B
get home late, and drop - pin' the ring in the spa - ghet - ti plate 'cause your
Am7 G/B C D G
hands are shak - in' so much. And it's the way that she looks with the rice

Bridge:

He said, "When you get home,__ she'll start__ __ to cry. When she says, 'I'm sor - ry,' say 'So am I.' And look in - to__ those eyes__ so__ deep in love,__ and drink it up,__ __ 'cause that's the

good stuff._____ Now, that's the

good stuff."_____

Verse 2:

He grabbed a carton of milk and he poured a glass.
And I smiled, and I said, "I'll have some of that."
We sat there and talked as an hour passed, like old friends.
I saw a black and white picture, and he caught my stare.
It was a pretty girl with bouffant hair.
He said, "That's my Bonnie, taken 'bout a year after we wed."
He said, "I spent five years in the bottle
When the cancer took her from me.
But I've been sober three years now,
'Cause the one thing stronger than the whiskey...

Chorus 2:

Was the sight of her holdin' our baby girl,
The way she adored that string of pearls
I gave her the day that our youngest boy Earl
Married his high school love.
And it's a new t-shirt, sayin' 'I'm a grandpa,'
Bein' right there as the time got small,
And holdin' her hand when the good Lord called her up.
Yeah, man, that's the good stuff."
(To Bridge:)

HOME

Words and Music by
MICHAEL BUBLÉ, ALAN CHANG
and AMY FOSTER

1. An-oth-er sum-mer day has come and gone a-way in Par-is and Rome,___ but I wan-na go home.___

Home - 6 - 1

HOW LONG

Words and Music by
J. D. SOUTHER

Moderately fast ♩ = 138

Verse 1:

1. Like a blue-bird_____ with his heart_____ re-moved_____ – lone-ly as a train_____ I've run just as far_____

Lyrics:

How_____ long, how_____ long?

Good-night, ba - by, rock____ your - self____ to sleep____ Sleep____ tight, ba - by, rock____

____ your - self____ to sleep____ B - b - b - bye - bye, ba - by, rock____ your - self____ to sleep.____

I RUN TO YOU

Words and Music by
CHARLES KELLEY, DAVE HAYWOOD,
HILLARY SCOTT and TOM DOUGLAS

Gtr. tuned down 1/2 step:
⑥ = E♭ ③ = G♭
⑤ = A♭ ② = B♭
④ = D♭ ① = E♭

Moderately ♩ = 112

I Run to You - 8 - 1

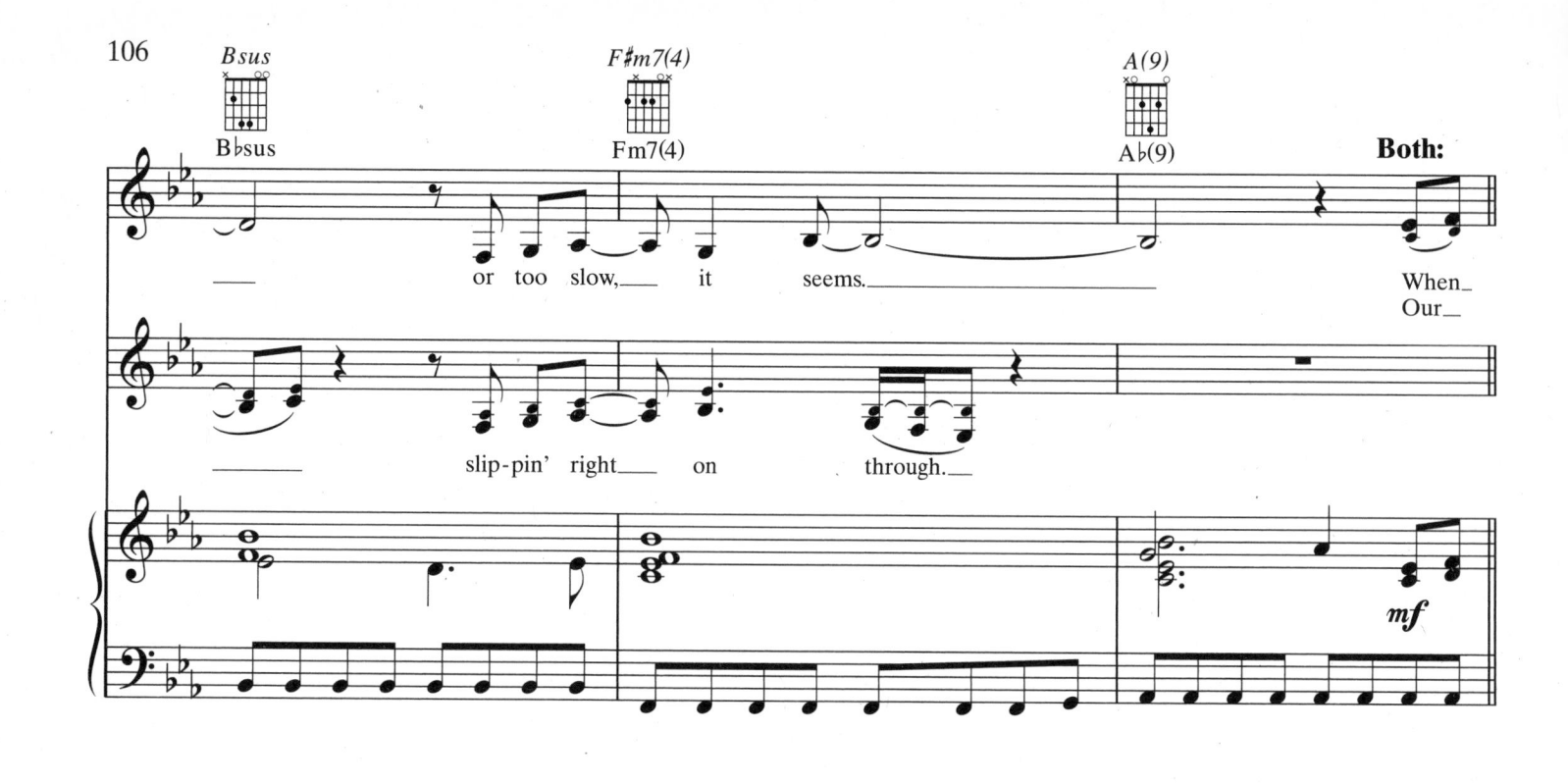

or too slow,___ it seems._____ When__ Our__

___ slip-pin' right___ on through.___

Both:

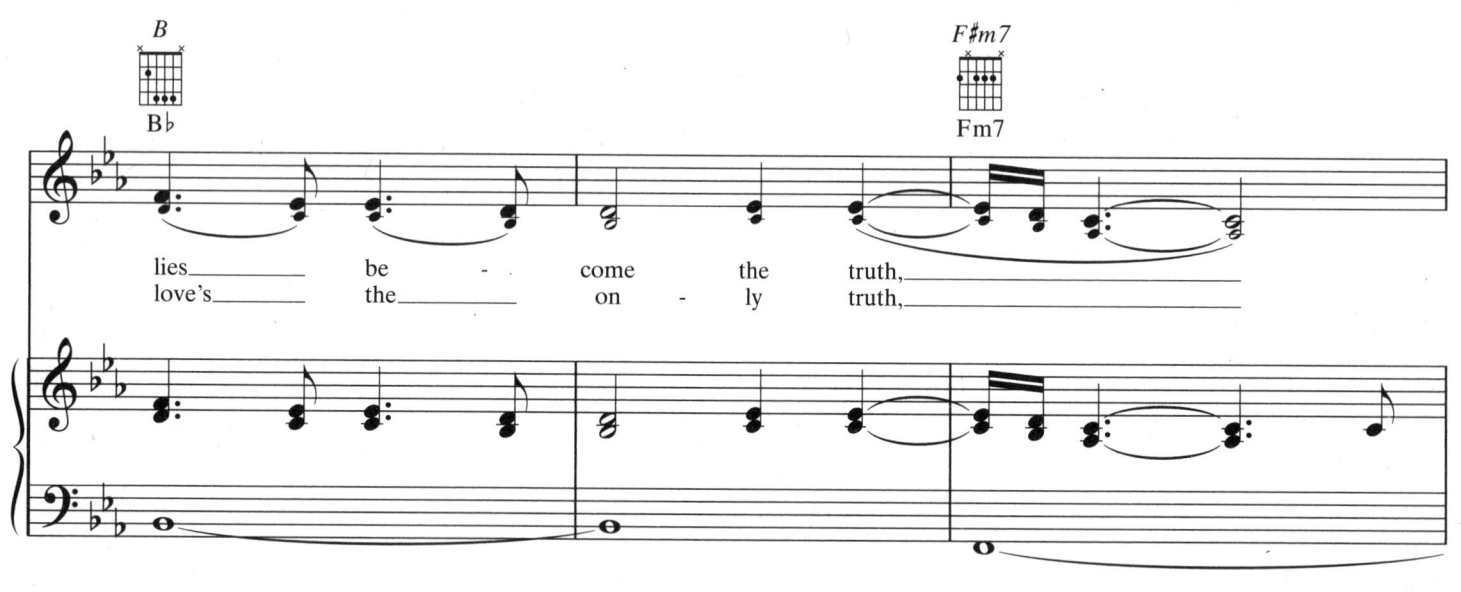

lies_____ be - come the truth,_____
love's_____ the_____ on - ly truth,_____

that's___ when_____ I_____ run to you.___
that's___ why_____ I_____ run to you.___

Chorus:

B/A
A
Bb/Ab
Ab
mp
Male:
I al - ways run to you.
Female:
Run to you.
Female:
Run to you.

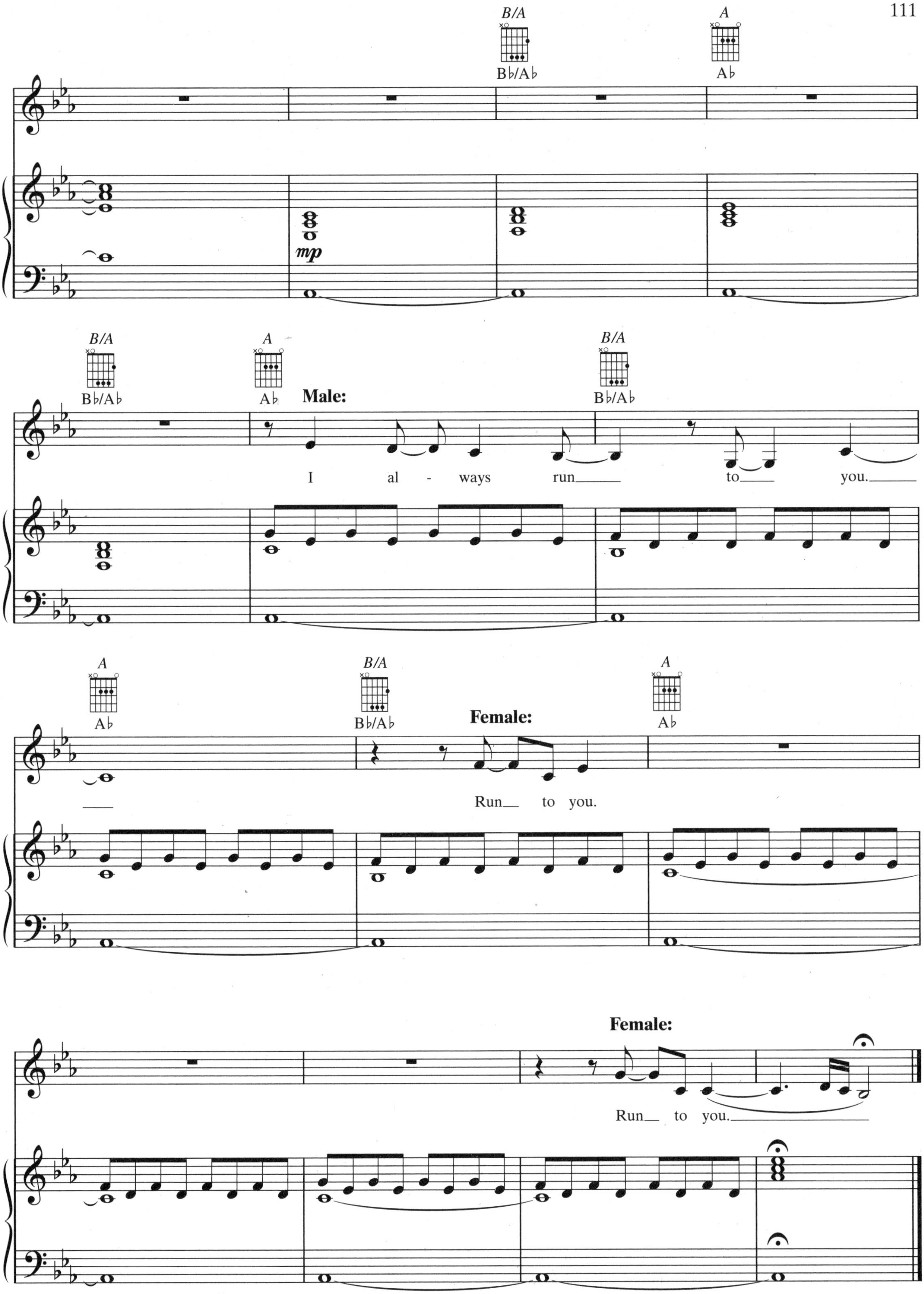

I TOLD YOU SO

Words and Music by
RANDY TRAVIS

I Told You So - 5 - 1

Lyrics:

tell me that__ you love me, too, and would we cry to-geth-er? Or
live and love__ for - ev - er and that I'm you're one and on - ly? Or

would you sim - ply laugh__ at me__ and say...
would you say__ the ta - bles fi - n'lly turned? Would you say I I

Chorus:

told you so,_____ oh, I told you so._____ I

told you some - day you'd_ come crawl - ing back__ and ask - ing me_____ to take_ you in.____

G G/D D7 C/G G C/G G Am/G G
Ab Ab/Eb Eb7 Db/Ab Ab Db/Ab Ab Bbm/Ab Ab
I told you so, but you
Bm C D/C C Bm Am7
Cm Db Eb/Db Db Cm Bbm7
had to go. Now I found some-bod-y new and you will
1.
D7 G
Eb7 Ab
nev-er break my heart in two a-gain.
dim.
mp
Bm G Bm7 Am7
Cm Ab Cm7 Bbm7
2. If I got

116

2.

D7 / G

Eb7 / Ab

nev-er break_ my heart_ in two a-gain.____

Am7

Bbm7

Now I found___ some-bod-y new___ and you___ will

D7 / G / Bm

Eb7 / Ab / Cm

nev-er break_ my heart_ in two a-gain.____

dim.

mp

G / Bm7 / Am7 / G

Ab / Cm7 / Bbm7 / Ab

molto rit.

8vb

IN MY DAUGHTER'S EYES

Words and Music by
JAMES SLATER

Bridge:

hand a-round my fin-ger, ah, it puts a smile__ in__ my heart.__ Ev-'ry-thing be -

comes a lit-tle clear-er. I re-al-ize what life__ is all a-bout. It's hang-ing on when your

heart has had__ e-nough. It's giv-ing more when you feel__ like giv-ing up.__ I've

seen the light.__ It's in my daugh - ter's eyes.

I WILL

Words and Music by
RORY LEE FEEK and DAVE PAHANISH

126

Bridge:

ev-er your day___ is done and still you feel you need some-one to hold___ you,___ I will.___

If you ev-er need to talk___ to some-bod-y who real-ly knows___ you,___ yes, I___

___ will,___ uh - huh.

D.S. % al Coda

I'll give up my life___

I Will - 6 - 5

I'LL JUST HOLD ON

Words and Music by
BEN HAYSLIP, BRYAN SIMPSON
and TROY OLSEN

I'll Just Hold On - 6 - 1

un-til you're_____ gone._____

Fmaj7 G 2. G

un - til_____

Am Em7 Am

_____you're gone.

Em7 F C G

Repeat ad lib. and fade

IN COLOR

Words and Music by
JAMES OTTO, JAMEY JOHNSON
and LEE MILLER

_____ you there?"_ He said, "Yeah, I was e - lev-en.

And times were tough_ back in_ Thir-ty - five._ That's me and Un-cle Joe just try'n' to sur - vive_ a cot-

ton farm in the Great De - pres - sion. 1. If it

Chorus 1:

looks like we were scared_ to death,_ like a cou-ple of kids_ just try-in' to save_ each oth-

C · G

Eb · Bb

er,   you should - a   seen   it   in____   col - or.____

Verse 2:

2. Ah,   and   this one   here__   was   tak - en   o - ver - seas__   in   the

dim.   ***mp***

F · C

Ab · Eb

mid - dle   of   hell__   in   Nine - teen__   For - ty - three__   in   the   win - ter - time;   you   can   al - most   see__   my__

G

Bb

____breath.   That   was   my   tail - gun - ner,   ol'   John - ny   Ma - gee;__   he   was   a

high-school teach-er from New Or-leans, and he had my back right through the day we

Chorus 2 & 3:

left. 2. If it looks like we were scared to death, like a

cou-ple of kids just try-in' to save each oth-er, you should-a seen it in col-

or. A pic-ture's worth a thou-sand words, but you

In Color - 8 - 4

right there in black_ and white._____ 3. And if it

cresc.

Coda

or._____ *(Inst. solo ad lib. behind vocal...*

You should - a seen it in___ col - or._____ Yeah, a

pic - ture's worth a thou - sand words,_ but you can't see what those shades_ of gray_ keep cov -

ered.   You should - a seen   it in____ col   -   or."_____

...end solo)

In Color - 8 - 8

IT'S FIVE O'CLOCK SOMEWHERE

Words and Music by
DONALD ROLLINS
and JIM BROWN

A D A

am I. | The work - day pass - es___ like___ mo - las - ses in win -
the night. | To - mor - row morn - ing___ I___ know there'll be hell

Bm A D G

ter - time, but it's Ju - ly.___ Get - tin' paid by the hour___ and
to pay, hey, but that's all right.___ I ain't had a day off now in

D A D

old - er by the min - ute. My boss just pushed___ me o - ver the lim - it. I'd like to
o - ver a year.___ My Ja - mai - can va - ca - tion's gon - na start right here. If the

G D A

call him some - thing. I think I'll just call it a day.___
phone's for me, you can tell them I just sailed a - way.___

Chorus:

but I don't care,___

and I don't care,___

it's five___ o'-clock some-where.

Repeat ad lib. and fade

(Dialogue - See additional lyrics)

Dialogue:
Jimmy: What time zone am I on? What country am I in?
Alan: It doesn't matter. It's five o'clock somewhere.
Jimmy: It's always on five in Margaritaville, come to think of it.
Alan: I heard that.
Jimmy: You've been there, haven't you?
Alan: Yes, sir.
Jimmy: I've seen your boat there.
Alan: I've been to Margaritaville a few times.
Jimmy: All right. That's good.
Alan: Stumbled my way back.
Jimmy: OK. Just want to make sure you can keep it between the navigational beacons.
Alan: Between the bouys. I got it.
Jimmy: All right. It's five o'clock. Let's go somewhere.
Alan: I'm ready. Crank it up.
Jimmy: Let's get out of here.
Alan: I'm gone.

JUST A DREAM

Words and Music by
HILLARY LINDSEY, STEVE McEWAN
and GORDIE SAMPSON

Just a Dream - 6 - 1

JUST GOT STARTED LOVIN' YOU

Words and Music by
D. VINCENT WILLIAMS, JIM FEMINO
and JAMES OTTO

Verses 1 & 2:

1. You don't have to go now, hon-ey, call 'em, tell 'em you won't be in to - day.____
2. What's the point in fight-in' what we're feel-in'? We both know we'll nev-er win.____

Ba - by, there ain't noth - in' at the of - fice so im - por - tant it can't
Ain't this what we're miss - in'? Let's just stop all this re - sist - in' and give

Just Got Started Lovin' You - 5 - 1

er felt this way. Girl,___ you're like a dream come true.___ Af - ter

all the love we've made, it sure___ would be a shame if we let this mo - ment end so___ soon.___

Verses 3 & 4:

{ 3. So, won't you lay back down be - side me, girl, just like I know you want___
{ 4. I'm thank - ful for the week - end, but two days in heav - en just ain't gon - na

to,___ mm.___ Trust me when I tell you, dar - lin'.
do.___ This is gon - na take for - ev - er, dar - lin'.

LIKE WE NEVER LOVED AT ALL

Words and Music by
JOHN RICH, VICKY McGEHEE
and SCOTT SACKS

Gtr. tuned down 1/2 step:
⑥ = E♭ ③ = G♭
⑤ = A♭ ② = B♭
④ = D♭ ① = E♭

LAST NAME

Words and Music by
CARRIE UNDERWOOD, HILLARY LINDSEY
and LUKE LAIRD

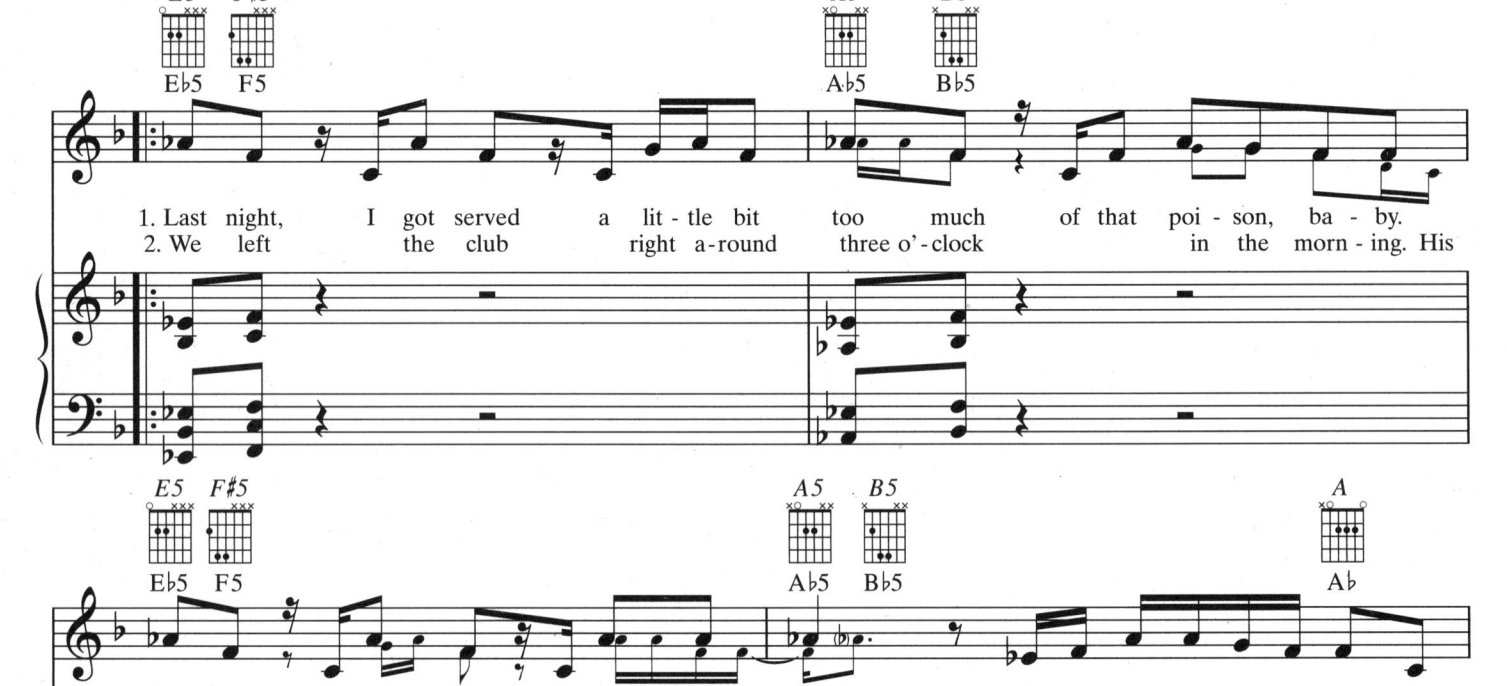

Moderately slow country rock ♩ = 80

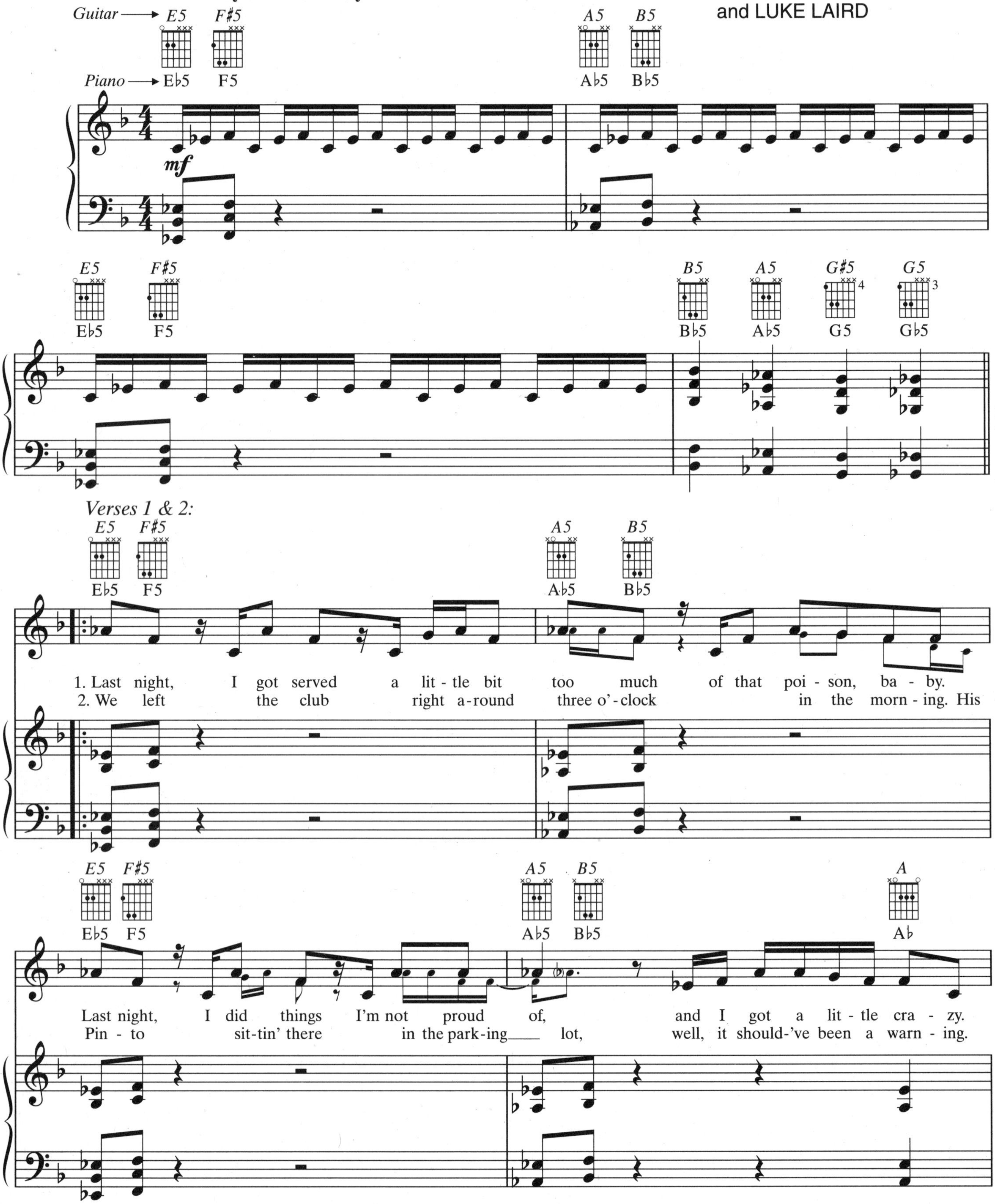
Guitar
E5 F♯5 A5 B5
Piano
E♭5 F5 A♭5 B♭5
mf
E5 F♯5 B5 A5 G♯5 G5
E♭5 F5 B♭5 A♭5 G5 G♭5
Verses 1 & 2:
E5 F♯5 A5 B5
E♭5 F5 A♭5 B♭5
1. Last night, I got served a lit - tle bit too much of that poi - son, ba - by.
2. We left the club right a-round three o'-clock in the morn - ing. His
E5 F♯5 A5 B5 A
E♭5 F5 A♭5 B♭5 A♭
Last night, I did things I'm not proud of, and I got a lit - tle cra - zy.
Pin - to sit-tin' there in the park-ing lot, well, it should-'ve been a warn - ing.

...end solo)

Verse 3:

3. To - day, I woke up think-in' 'bout El - vis, some-where in Ve - gas. I'm not sure

how I got here or how this ring on my left hand just ap - peared_ out of

no - where. I got-ta go. I take the chips and the Pin - to and hit the road._ They say what

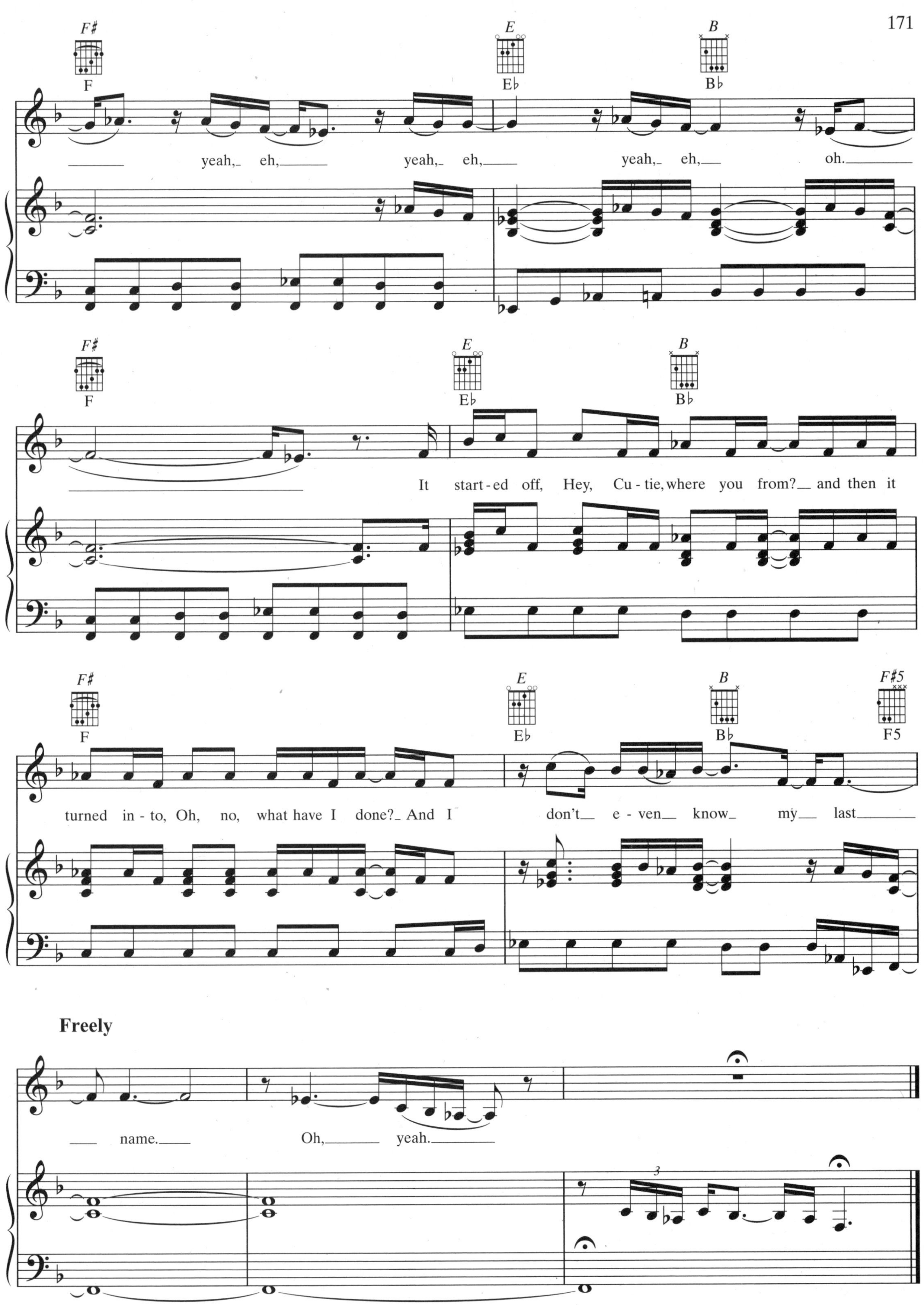
F♯ F
E E♭
B B♭
yeah, eh, yeah, eh, yeah, eh, oh.
It start-ed off, Hey, Cu-tie, where you from? and then it
turned in-to, Oh, no, what have I done? And I
don't e-ven know my last
F♯5 F5
Freely
name. Oh, yeah.

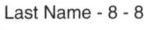

LIVE LIKE YOU WERE DYING

Words and Music by
TIM NICHOLS and
CRAIG WISEMAN

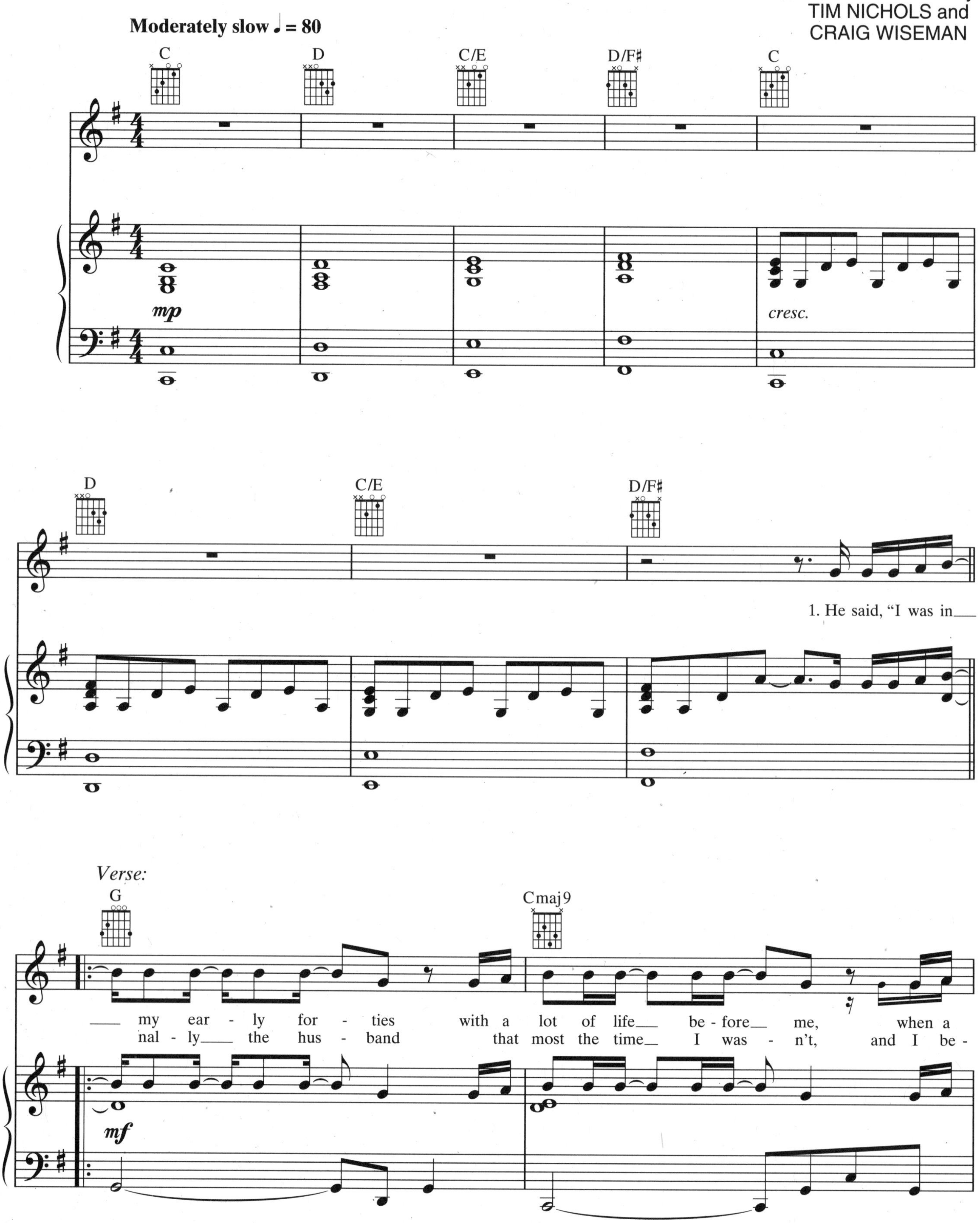

Moderately slow ♩ = 80

Verse:

my ear-ly for-ties with a lot of life__ be-fore__ me, when a
nal-ly__ the hus-band that most the time__ I was-n't, and I be-

1. He said, "I was in__

Live Like You Were Dying - 7 - 1

175

Live Like You Were Dying - 7 - 4

"Some - day,___ I hope___ you___ get the chance to live___ like you were dy -

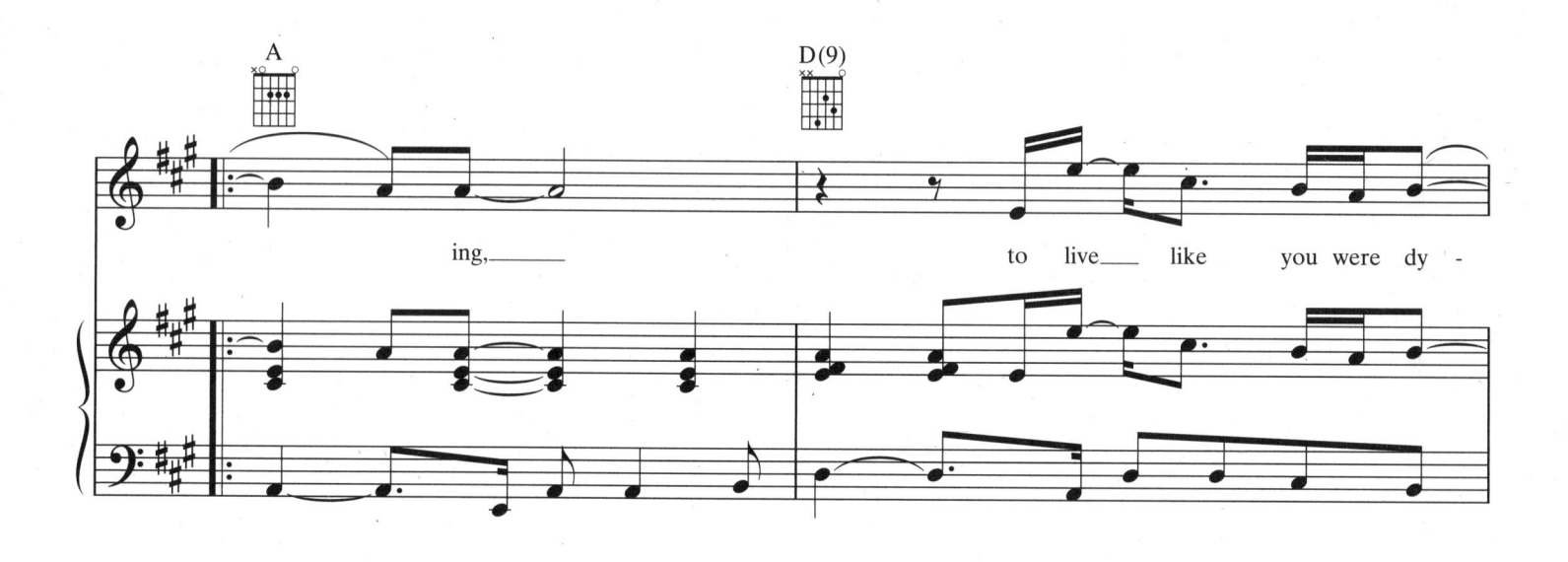

ing,_____ to live___ like you were dy -

Repeat ad lib. and fade

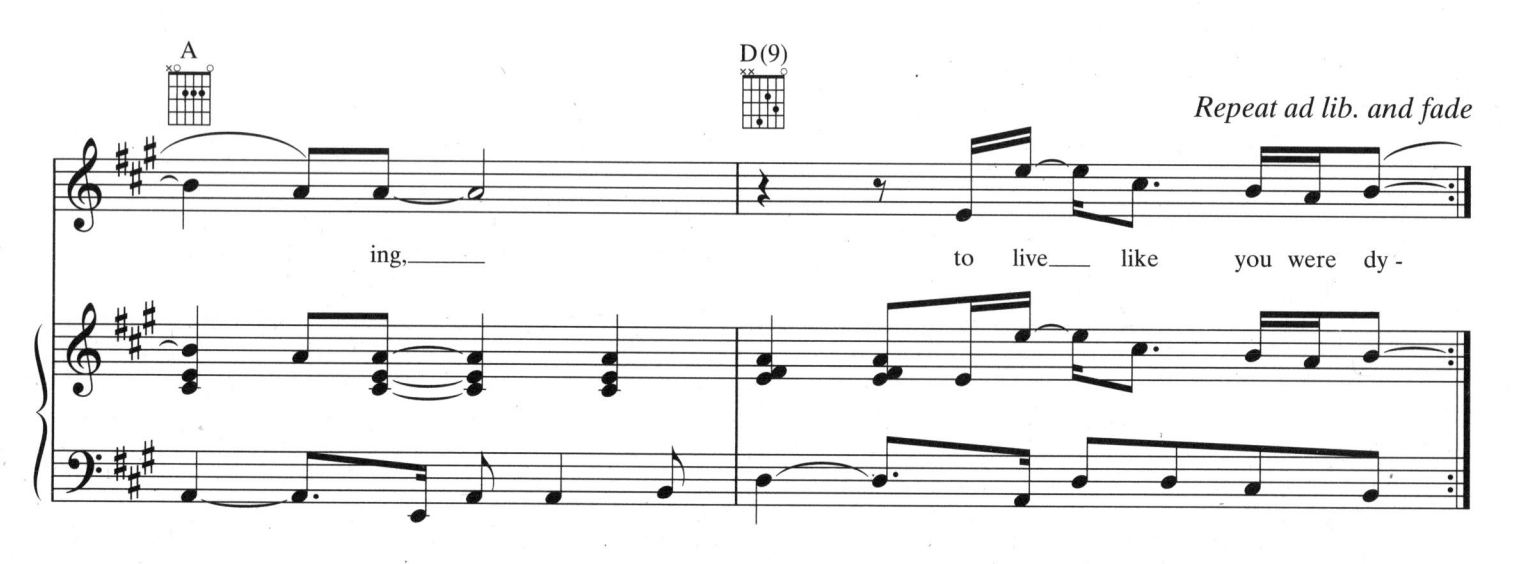

ing,_____ to live___ like you were dy -

LOST IN THIS MOMENT

Words and Music by
JOHN RICH, RODNEY CLAWSON
and KEITH ANDERSON

Slowly ♩ = 76

(with pedal)

Verse 1:

1. I see your ma-ma and the can-dles and the tears and ro - ses.___

I see your dad-dy walk his daugh-ter down the aisle.___

And my knees start to trem-ble as I tell the preach - er,___ "Don't she look___ beau-ti - ful___

Verses 2 & 3:

2. All the won-der-ful___ words   in my head I've been___ think-ing,—
3. *See additional lyrics*

you know, I wan-na say them all   just   right.___

I lift your veil, and an-gels___ start sing-ing.___   Such a heav - en - ly___

Verse 3:
I smell the jasmine floating in the air like a love song,
Watch my words draw sweet tears from your eyes.
Bow our heads while the preacher talks to Jesus,
Please bless this brand-new life, yeah.
(To Chorus:)

LOVE DON'T LIVE HERE

Words and Music by
DAVID WESLEY HAYWOOD,
CHARLES KELLEY and HILLARY SCOTT

C(9)
Db(9)
G
Ab
F6/9
Gb6/9
1.
to get back what is gone.
oh, and I would curse your name.
But I'm
2.
Hey!
Verses 2 & 3:
2. Well, I heard the news
you can try
that you were back in town
to tell me how it is,
and just
and try to

C(9)
Db(9)

||2. G
Ab

N.C.

3. Well, ba-by, ___ oh, no. ___ That love

___ don't live ___ here an - y - more. ___

G
Ab

F6/9
Gb6/9

C(9)
Db(9)

Whoa, no, ___ no.   Sug-ar, no,

G
Ab

F6/9
Gb6/9

C(9)
Db(9)

G
Ab

F6/9
Gb6/9

___ no.   You don't live ___ here an -

NEED YOU NOW

Words and Music by
DAVE HAYWOOD, CHARLES KELLEY,
HILLARY SCOTT and JOSH KEAR

*Alternate between open G and A on the 3rd string.

Need You Now - 7 - 1

MISSISSIPPI GIRL

Words and Music by
JOHN RICH and
ADAM SHOENFELD

Moderately slow (♩ = 84)

Verse 1:

1. Well, it's a long way____ from Star,____ Mis-sis-sip - pi,____ to the big stage____ I'm sing-in' on____ to-night.____ And some - times,____ the but-ter-flies____ still get me when I'm

Mississippi Girl - 6 - 1

just 'cause ev-'ry-bod-y knows her name.___ Ain't big - head-ed from a lit - tle bit of fame.___

___ I still like wear-in' my old ball cap,

rid - in' my kids a - round___ pig - gy-*back*. They might know me all a - round___ the world,___

___ but, y'all, I'm still___ a Mis - sis-sip - pi girl.___

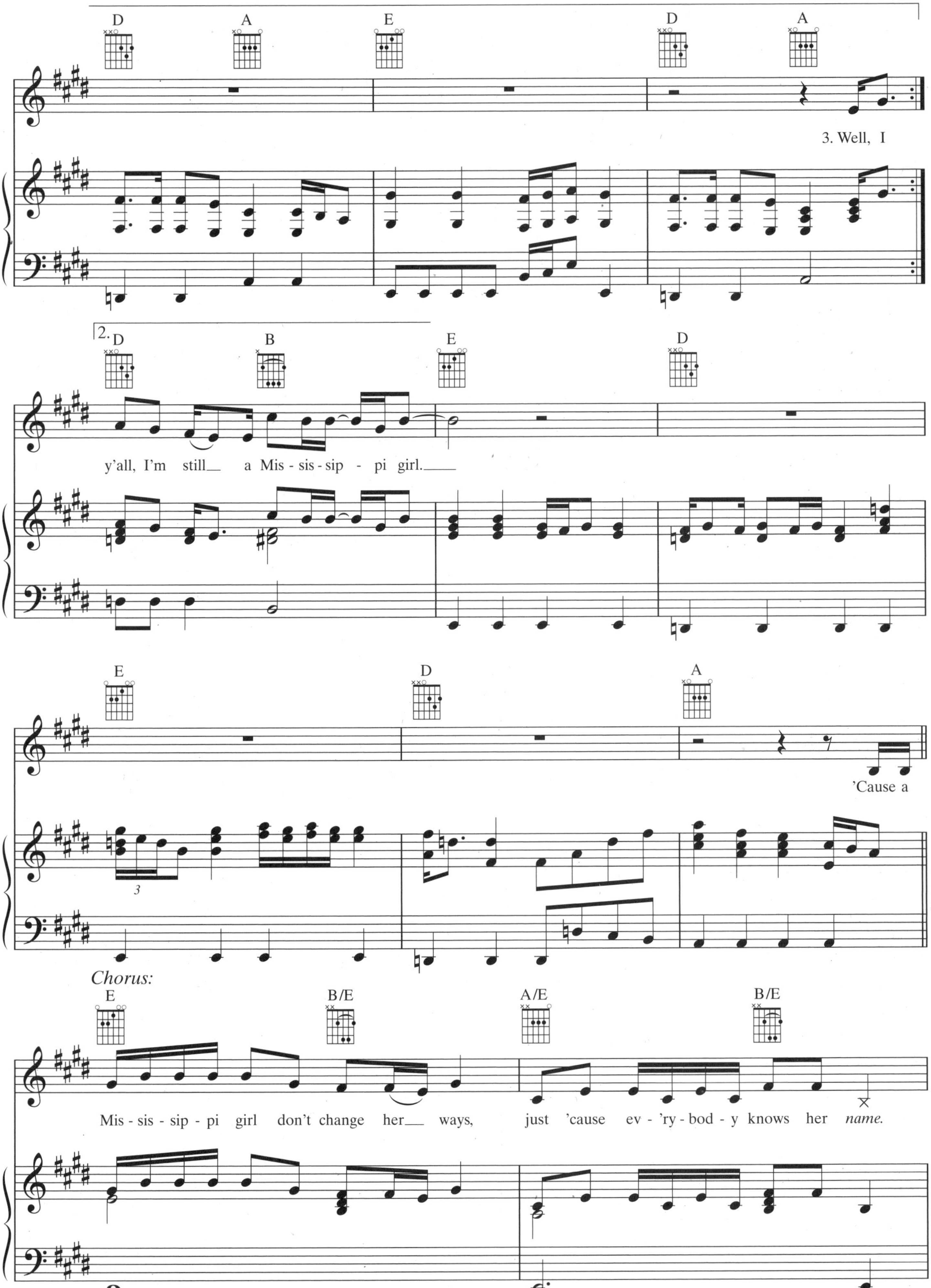
D A E D A
3. Well, I
2. D B E D
y'all, I'm still__ a Mis-sis-sip - pi girl.__
E D A
'Cause a
Chorus:
E B/E A/E B/E
Mis-sis-sip-pi girl don't change her__ ways, just 'cause ev - 'ry-bod - y knows her name.

Repeat ad lib. and fade

NOT READY TO MAKE NICE

Words and Music by
EMILY ROBISON, MARTIE MAGUIRE,
NATALIE MAINES and DAN WILSON

Slowly ♩ = 80

*Original recording in F♯ major with guitar tuned down a half step.

Not Ready to Make Nice - 7 - 1

Lyrics:

"Can't you just get o-ver it?" It turned my whole world a-round, and I kind-a like it. I've made my bed, and I sleep like a ba-by with no re-grets, and I don't mind say-in' it's a sad, sad sto-ry when a moth-er will teach her daugh-ter that she ought-a hate a per-fect strang-er. And how

Chorus:

read - y to make__ nice, I'm not read - y to back__ down. I'm still

mad as hell__ and I don't have time__ to go__ 'round and 'round__ and 'round.__ It's too

late to make__ it right.__ I prob-'bly would-n't, if__ I could.__ 'Cause I'm

1.

mad as hell,__ can't bring__ my - self__ to do__ what it is__ you think__ I should.__

PROUD OF THE HOUSE WE BUILT

Words and Music by
MARV GREEN, RONNIE DUNN
and TERRY McBRIDE

up - hill bat - tle near - ly ev - 'ry day. Look-in'
close my eyes___ at night and I still feel___ the same

1.
back, I would - n't have it an - y oth - er way. I'm

To Next Strain

2.
fire in my heart_ I felt out in that field._____ I'm

Chorus:
proud of the house_ we___ built.___ It's strong - er than sticks,_ stones, and steel._

Chorus:

SHUTTIN' DETROIT DOWN

Words and Music by
JOHN RICH and
J.D. ANDERSON

Moderately fast ♩ = 84

...end solo) Yeah, while they're liv-in' it up___ on Wall___

___ Street in that New York Cit-y town, here in the real___ world,___ they're

224

SOMEBODY LIKE YOU

Words and Music by
JOHN SHANKS and KEITH URBAN

Moderately ♩ = 112

1. There's a

new wind blow-in' like I've nev-er known._ I'm breath-in' deep-er than I've

2.–5. *See additional lyrics*

Somebody Like You - 5 - 1

Verse 2:
Well, I'm letting go of all my lonely yesterdays
And forgiving myself for the mistakes I've made.
Now there's just one thing, the only thing I wanna do.
I wanna love somebody, love somebody like you.
(To Bridge:)

Verse 3:
I used to run in circles, goin' nowhere fast.
I'd take one step forward, end up two steps back.
I couldn't walk a straight line even if I wanted to,
But I wanna love somebody, love somebody like you.

Verse 4:
Instrumental solo
(To Bridge:)

Verse 5:
Sometimes it's hard for me to understand,
But you're teachin' me to be a better man.
Don't want to take this life for granted like I used to do.
I wanna love somebody, love somebody like you.
(To Coda)

SMALL TOWN USA

Words and Music by
JEREMY STOVER, BRIAN MAHER
and JUSTIN MOORE

bod - y knows me and I___ know_ them,__ and I be - lieve that's the way we were s'pposed to live.__ I would-n't

trade_ one sin - gle day____ here in small town U. S.__ A.____ 1. Give me a

Chorus 1 & 2:

Sat - ur - day night,__ my ba - by by my side, a lit - tle Hank Ju - nior and a six-pack of light,} an
(2.) Sat - ur - day night,__ my ba - by by my side,____ Da - vid Al - len Coe__ and a six-pack of light,}

old dirt road____ and I'll be just fine.____ Give me a

234

SO SMALL

Words and Music by
CARRIE UNDERWOOD, HILLARY LINDSEY
and LUKE LAIRD

So Small - 8 - 1

So Small - 8 - 4

yeah, yeah, yeah, yeah._____ 'Cause some -

times_____ that moun - tain you've_ been climb - ing is just a grain_ of_____

___ sand._____ And what

you've been out__ there search - ing for__ for - ev - er is in___ your___

WATCHING YOU

Words and Music by
RODNEY ATKINS, STEVE DEAN
and BRIAN WHITE

Moderately fast country ♩ = 138

(with pedal)

Verse:

1. Driv-in' through town, just my boy and me,__ with a "Hap-py Meal"__ in his boost-er seat,__
2. *See additional lyrics*

know-in' that he could-n't have the toy 'til his nug-gets were gone,__ a

Watching You - 6 - 1

Chorus 1 & 2:

1. He said, "I've been watch-ing you, Dad, ain't that cool? I'm your buck-a-roo; I want to
2. *See additional lyrics*

be like you. And eat all my food and grow as tall as you are.

We got cow-boy boots and cam - o pants. Yeah, we're just a-like, hey, ain't

we, Dad? I want to do ev-'ry-thing you do;

Chorus 3:

'Cause I've been_ watch-ing you,__ Dad, ain't___ that cool?__ I'm your buck-a-roo;__ I want to be like you.__ And eat all___ my food__ and grow as tall__ as you__ are. By then I'll be strong as Su-per-man.__ We'll be just a-like,__ hey, won't__ we, Dad,__ when I can do__ ev-'ry-thing__ you do?_____

Verse 2:
We got back home and I went to the barn.
I bowed my head and I prayed real hard,
Said, "Lord, please help me help my stupid self."
Just this side of bedtime later that night,
Turnin' on my son's Scooby-Doo night-light.
He crawled out of bed and he got down on his knees.
He closed his little eyes, folded his little hands,
Spoke to God like he was talkin' to a friend.
And I said, "Son, now where'd you learn to pray like that?"
(To Chorus 2:)

Chorus 2:
He said, "I've been watching you, Dad, ain't that cool?
I'm your buckaroo; I want to be like you.
And eat all my food and grow as tall as you are.
We like fixin' things and holding Mama's hand,
Yeah, we're just alike, hey, ain't we, Dad?
I want to do everything you do; so I've been watching you."
(To Bridge:)

THEN

Words and Music by
CHRIS DuBOIS, ASHLEY GORLEY
and BRAD PAISLEY